TALES OF HORROR
VAMPIRES

by Jim Pipe

BEARPORT
PUBLISHING

Credits

Amit Gogia CyberMedia Services: 16, 25; Denmark: 23; Jaime Duplass: 20; Neo Edmund: 20–21; FLPA: 14–15; Lerner Gerardo: 17; Jakez: 22–23; Magdalena Kucova: 12; Iryna Kurhan: 11; Erich Lessing/Art Resource, NY: 18; Mansker: 28; Michael Marquand: 7; Ioan Nicolae: 18–19; Vladimir Pomortzeff: 31; Shutterstock: 6–7, 9, 10–11, 13, 15, 24, 26; ticktock Media archive: Cover, Title Page, 4, 5, 8, 27, 28–29, 30.

Every effort has been made to trace the copyright holders and we apologize in advance for any unintentional omissions. We would be pleased to insert the appropriate acknowledgment in any subsequent edition of this publication.

Library of Congress Cataloging-in-Publication Data

Pipe, Jim, 1966–
  Vampires / by Jim Pipe.
      p. cm. — (Tales of horror)
  Includes index.
  ISBN-13: 978-1-59716-205-0 (library binding)
  ISBN-10: 1-59716-205-1 (library binding)
  ISBN-13: 978-1-59716-212-8 (pbk.)
  ISBN-10: 1-59716-212-4 (pbk.)
  1. Vampires—Juvenile literature. I. Title. II. Series: Pipe, Jim, 1966– Tales of horror.

  BF1556.P55 2007
  398'.45—dc22

                    2006013656

For more information, write to Bearport Publishing Company, Inc., 101 Fifth Avenue, Suite 6R, New York, New York 10003. Printed in the United States of America.

10 9 8 7 6 5 4 3 2 1

The Tales of Horror series was originally developed by ticktock Media Ltd.

Table of Contents

Creatures of the Night

Beware of vampires! They are looking to sink their **fangs** into their next victims.

Vampires are **corpses** that have come back to life with **supernatural** powers. During the day, vampires rest in their **graves** or in **coffins**. At night, however, these creatures search for the food they need to stay alive—blood.

For hundreds of years, frightening vampire stories have haunted people all over the world. Nowadays, few people believe vampires actually exist. Yet **legends** of vampires can still give readers the chills! If you are brave enough, read on to find out more about these bloodsuckers.

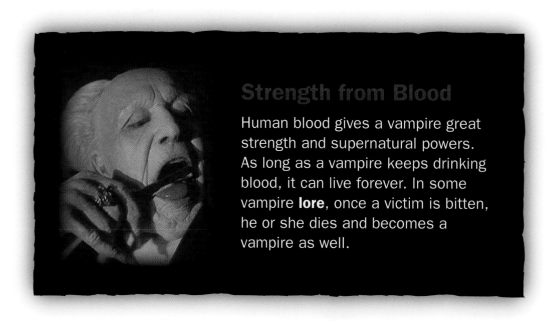

Strength from Blood

Human blood gives a vampire great strength and supernatural powers. As long as a vampire keeps drinking blood, it can live forever. In some vampire **lore**, once a victim is bitten, he or she dies and becomes a vampire as well.

The Vampire Look

Vampires come in all shapes and sizes. People who are looking for vampires should watch for creatures with long, curling fingernails, pale skin, and rat-like fangs.

According to some legends, a vampire is tall and elegant. Other legends describe the vampire as a kind of short, sweaty **zombie** that smells horrible. These sweaty vampires have scary faces covered in filth, and red, glowing eyes.

When vampires are worried that they might be discovered, they can change the way they look, or "shape-shift." They may turn into bats, wolves, or even mist.

No Cape for These Vampires

In some parts of the world, vampires never look like humans at all. They are monsters in the shape of cats or spiders.

Vampire Powers

Vampires have many supernatural powers. Their bodies can move faster than the human eye can follow. They can climb walls like lizards. They can even communicate, mind to mind, with fellow vampires. These powers help them as they search for blood and battle vampire hunters.

Of all the vampire's powers, however, the ability to **hypnotize** others is the most chilling. People who stare too long into a vampire's cold, glassy eyes will soon become victims. Against their will, these poor people will find themselves moving toward the monster!

Forces of Nature

In some legends, vampires have great power over nature. They can control wind and rain. Vampires can also make great swarms of rats attack their enemies.

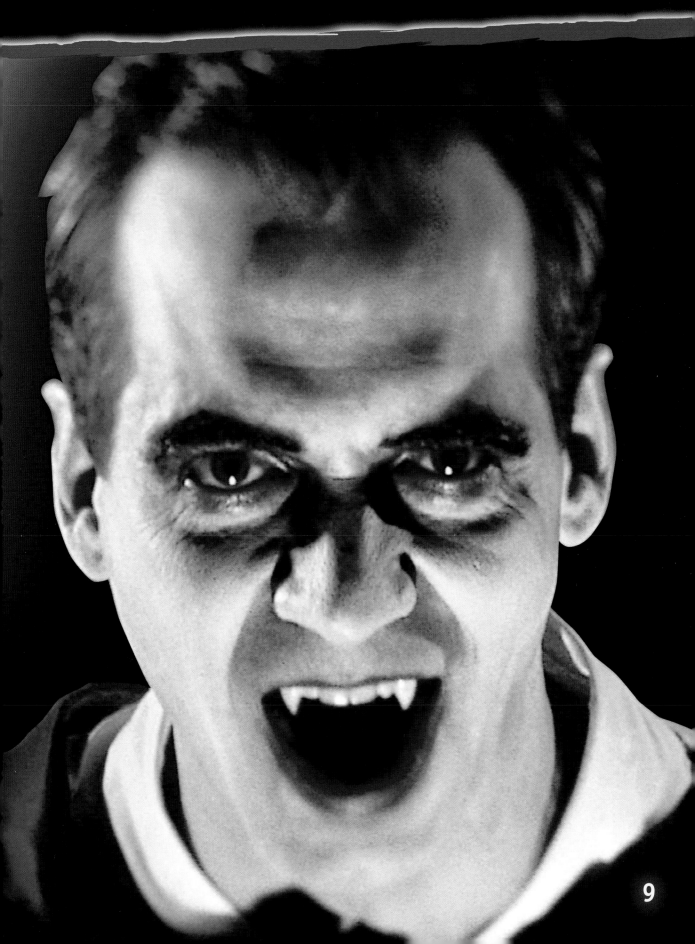

Vampire Weaknesses

Vampires have amazing strengths. Yet they have weaknesses, too. In some legends, a vampire cannot enter a house unless invited. In addition, direct sunlight can burn or kill these creatures. To avoid the sun's rays, vampires sleep during the day. They prefer to be at rest in their coffins well before sunrise. Even at night, vampires prefer rooms lit only with candles.

Vampires also must be close to soil from their home country. When traveling, a vampire usually brings along a coffin filled with the soil. The vampire cannot sleep without it.

Is It a Vampire?

To surprise their victims, vampires often try to pass themselves off as ordinary human beings. Two weaknesses can give them away, however. Vampires don't cast shadows, and they have no reflections in mirrors and glass!

Back Off, Bloodsucker!

People have come up with many different ways to protect themselves from vampires. The most popular methods have always included garlic. People wear garlic bulbs around their necks. They also place the bulbs near doors and windows. These practices probably grew out of an ancient European belief that garlic has magical powers against all kinds of evil.

There are many other ways to guard against these bloodsuckers. In vampire stories, people often hold up religious symbols in front of the creature. Children in Malaysia once wore silk armbands to protect themselves against a vampire called the *bajang*. The ancient Romanians believed that socks stolen from a dead person were a powerful (if smelly) way to keep vampires at a distance.

Out for the Count

In Serbia, people leave a pile of poppy seeds near a vampire's grave. Why? When the vampire rises, the bloodsucker won't be able to walk past the seeds without counting them. A big enough pile will keep a vampire busy all night.

Hunting Vampires

One thing is certain: a vampire hunter's task is not easy. Finding a vampire is tough, but killing it is even tougher.

To find one of these creatures, some hunters lead a horse around a **graveyard** or old castle. If the horse gets spooked, it has gotten too close to a vampire's coffin.

When hunters dig up a corpse, they look for blood around the mouth, long **talon**-like fingernails, and fangs. If they see these signs, they know they've found one of the undead.

To kill the evil creature, the hunter must drive a **wooden stake** through its heart. Then he or she has to cut off the head and burn the body to keep the vampire from coming back.

Special Cases

Some vampires need to be killed in special ways. Female Indian vampires, called *Yakshis*, can only be killed with an iron nail through their head.

Polish vampires, called *Upiers*, must be burned. While on fire, their bodies burst and hundreds of **maggots** and rats pour out. Each of these creatures must also be killed to make sure the vampire doesn't return.

Vampire Scares

Sometimes people have believed their village was under attack by vampires. Then they panicked and did foolish things to defend themselves.

In 1725, a mysterious illness started killing people in a Serbian village. First, a man named Peter Plogojowitz died. A week later, more people died. The villagers thought Peter had turned into a vampire and was killing people! They dug up his body and thrust a sharp stake through his heart.

A wave of vampire stories swept across Eastern Europe in the 1700s. Terrified villagers began digging up bodies and burning them. In some areas, mobs went on vampire hunts. They killed hundreds of innocent people.

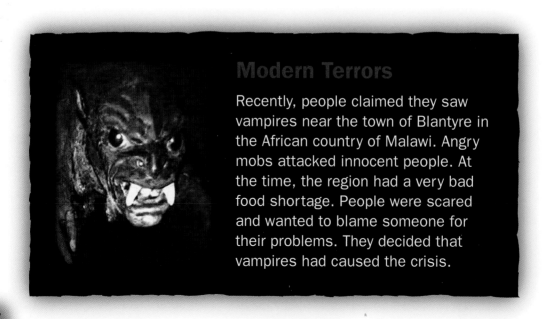

Modern Terrors

Recently, people claimed they saw vampires near the town of Blantyre in the African country of Malawi. Angry mobs attacked innocent people. At the time, the region had a very bad food shortage. People were scared and wanted to blame someone for their problems. They decided that vampires had caused the crisis.

The First Dracula

Prince Vlad Dracula (1431–1476) ruled a part of Romania called Walachia. This part of Europe is one of the places where vampire **myths** first began.

In Romanian, the word "Dracul" means *dragon* or *devil.* Prince Vlad certainly lived up to the meaning of his name. He was famous for sticking long, sharp stakes through his enemies' bodies. He supposedly even ate bread dipped in their blood. He chopped off the heads of lords. He even killed women and children.

Although he wasn't a real vampire, Vlad was extremely cruel. Hundreds of years later, his name would be used for the most famous vampire of all time.

Dracula the Vampire Hunter

Prince Vlad Dracula is actually considered a hero in Romania. He helped defend his people and land from invaders. In fact, there are legends of Prince Vlad *hunting* vampires!

19

A World of Vampires

Vampires from different parts of the world often look different from one another. They also may have unique powers:

- *Lagaroo*, a vampire from the Caribbean island of Grenada, looks like a sweet grandmother during the day. At night, however, she becomes a flying ball of flame looking for blood.
- *Asanbosam* lives deep in the forests of western Africa. It looks human but has iron teeth and hooks on its legs.
- *Manananggal*, from the Philippines, looks like a beautiful woman. When it's time to feed, however, the top half of her body separates from the bottom half and flies into the night!

Ancient Monsters

Some vampire legends have been around for a very long time. The ancient Greeks believed in the *Lamia*. She was a vampire who stole little children so that she could drink their blood. Her snake-like body had a human female's head. In some stories, she could take her eyes out and put them back in again!

21

Unusual Bloodsuckers

Some vampires appear as humans most of the time. Other vampires spend time in different forms. They may appear as plants or animals. Some even take the form of chairs, houses, cars, motorcycles, and ships!

In Bosnian folklore, watermelons and pumpkins kept more than ten days after Christmas can become vampires. Luckily, these fruits have no teeth!

In Asian stories, vampires can **transform** themselves into butterflies. This idea may be based on a real-life insect. The Asian vampire moth, which has no teeth, sucks blood from deer and water buffalo.

Real-Life Vampires

Some vampire stories are based on real bloodsucking animals. For example, vampire bats really exist. They live in South America and feed on sleeping pigs, cows, horses, and, very rarely, people! They bite a soft area on the skin and then lap up the blood with their tongues.

Bram Stoker's *Dracula*

In 1897, Irish writer Bram Stoker came out with his shocking novel *Dracula*. The book, which Stoker almost called *The Un-Dead*, introduced the vampire Count Dracula to the world. Some people believe that the character is based on Prince Vlad.

Stoker invented new powers for vampires. Dracula could turn into green mist. He could walk about in daylight and not turn to dust.

In the novel, Dracula leaves his castle in Transylvania and sails to London. Once in England, he begins to turn new victims into vampires.

Vampire hunter Dr. Van Helsing and his friends eventually drive Dracula back to Transylvania. They kill the monster with a knife—not a wooden stake—through the heart!

Vampire Technology

The heroes of *Dracula* use technology that was cutting edge in **Victorian** times. They chase Dracula across Europe on **steamships** and trains. They also use the **telegraph** to send messages to each other about Dracula's location.

Dracula from the
1992 movie,
Bram Stoker's Dracula

25

Other Vampire Tales

Bram Stoker is just one of hundreds of authors who have written about vampires. The first vampire books came out during the vampire hunts of the 1700s. They read like science reports. In 1746, a French monk named Dom Augustin Calmet wrote the most famous of these reports. It was a study of vampires in Eastern Europe, the part of the world where Dracula came from.

Before Bram Stoker was even born, John William Polidori wrote *The Vampyre* (1819). This novel started a vampire **craze**. It also introduced a new idea about vampires. In old folktales, vampires were always peasants. The main character in Polidori's book, however, was **aristocratic**. After Polidori's book came out, many other writers began to make their vampires aristocratic, too.

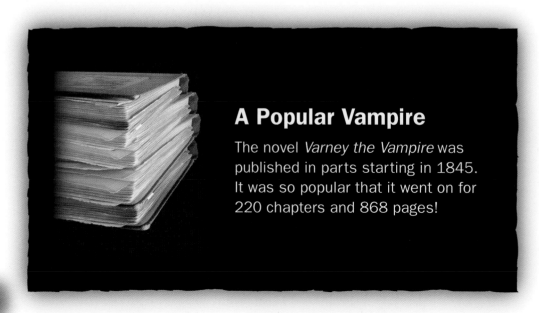

A Popular Vampire

The novel *Varney the Vampire* was published in parts starting in 1845. It was so popular that it went on for 220 chapters and 868 pages!

Movie and Television Vampires

Vampire stories make exciting movies! F. W. Murnau made the first vampire film, *Nosferatu,* in 1922. He based it on Bram Stoker's book *Dracula.* The movie inspired hundreds of other people to make vampire movies and television shows.

Movies and TV shows often combine old myths with new ideas about vampires. In *Buffy the Vampire Slayer*, for example, Buffy Summers is a high-kicking **martial arts** expert. She uses her high kicks in battles with the undead. However, she still uses an old-fashioned stake to kill vampires.

My Funny Vampire

Not all vampire movies are thrillers. *The Fearless Vampire Killers; or: Pardon Me, But Your Teeth Are in My Neck* (1967) is a comedy that makes fun of other vampire stories. In the film, the vampire hunters are clumsy, and the local inn is decorated with loads of garlic.

Do Vampires Exist?

Throughout history, people have blamed mysterious deaths on supernatural forces. For example, in 1727, four people in a Serbian village died. Villagers believed the dead were the victims of a man named Arnold Paole—a neighbor whom they thought had become a vampire. When they dug up Paole's corpse, they found blood in the coffin. When they drove a stake through his heart, they heard a groan!

Science may explain both of these "supernatural" findings, however. The blood was probably from Paole's rotting body. The groan might have been the sound of gases escaping from the bloated corpse.

Today, most people don't believe in vampires. They look to science to solve unusual mysteries. Yet almost everyone still loves the thrill of imagining a creature that sucks blood and lives forever.

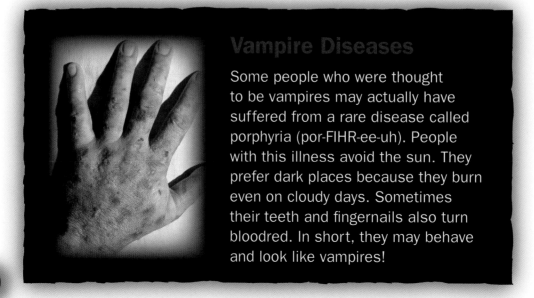

Vampire Diseases

Some people who were thought to be vampires may actually have suffered from a rare disease called porphyria (por-FIHR-ee-uh). People with this illness avoid the sun. They prefer dark places because they burn even on cloudy days. Sometimes their teeth and fingernails also turn bloodred. In short, they may behave and look like vampires!

Glossary

aristocratic (uh-*riss*-tuh-KRAT-ik) coming from a rich and sometimes noble family

coffins (KAWF-inz) long boxes used to hold dead bodies

corpses (KORPS-iz) dead bodies

craze (KRAZE) when a group of people become excited or worried about the same thing

fangs (FANGZ) long, pointed teeth

graves (GRAYVZ) holes dug into the ground where dead people are buried

graveyard (GRAYV-yard) an area of land where dead people are buried

hypnotize (HIP-nuh-*tize*) to control another person's mind by putting them in a trance

legends (LEJ-uhnds) stories that are handed down from the past and are generally believed to be true by those who tell them

lore (LOR) a collection of traditional stories

maggots (MAG-uhts) flies at the early, worm-like stage of their life cycle

martial arts (MAR-shuhl ARTS) forms of self-defense, such as karate and judo, that come from Asia

myths (MITHS) traditional stories that often tell of larger-than-life beings and mysterious events

steamships (STEEM-ships) boats that run on energy from steam

supernatural (*soo*-pur-NACH-ur-uhl) something unusual that breaks the laws of nature

talon (TAL-uhn) a sharp claw

telegraph (TEL-uh-graf) a way to send messages through wires using a code

transform (transs-FORM) to change into something else

Victorian (vik-TOR-ee-uhn) from the period when England was ruled by Queen Victoria (1837–1901)

wooden stake (WUD-uhn STAYK) a piece of wood with a sharp point at the end

zombie (ZOM-bee) a dead body that rises out of the grave in a trance

Index